LUCY CHASES MICE ON THE LOOSE,

AND TOM? HE KEEPS SIPPING HIS JUICE.

Supported by Latvian Writers' Union (*Latvijas Rakstnieku Savienība*)
and Ministry of Culture of the Republic of Latvia

   Latvijas Rakstnieku savienība   Latvia 100

First published in the UK in 2018 by the Emma Press, Birmingham
Originally published in 2013 as "Darbiņi sajūk" by Liels un mazs, Rīga, Latvia

Text © Maija Laukmane, 2006
English-language translation © Žanete Vēvere Pasqualini and Kate Wakeling, 2018
Illustrations © Sabine Moore, 2013

BICKI-BOOKS
Artistic director – Rūta Briede
Design – Rūta Briede and Artis Briedis

Printed in Latvia by *Talsu tipogrāfija*
on *Scandia 2000 Natural* 150 gsm and *Scandia 2000 Natural* 300 gsm

A CIP catalogue record of this book is available from the British Library
All rights reserved.

ISBN 978-1-910139-95-0
theemmapress.com